Prison Segmentation
For
Joint Ventures

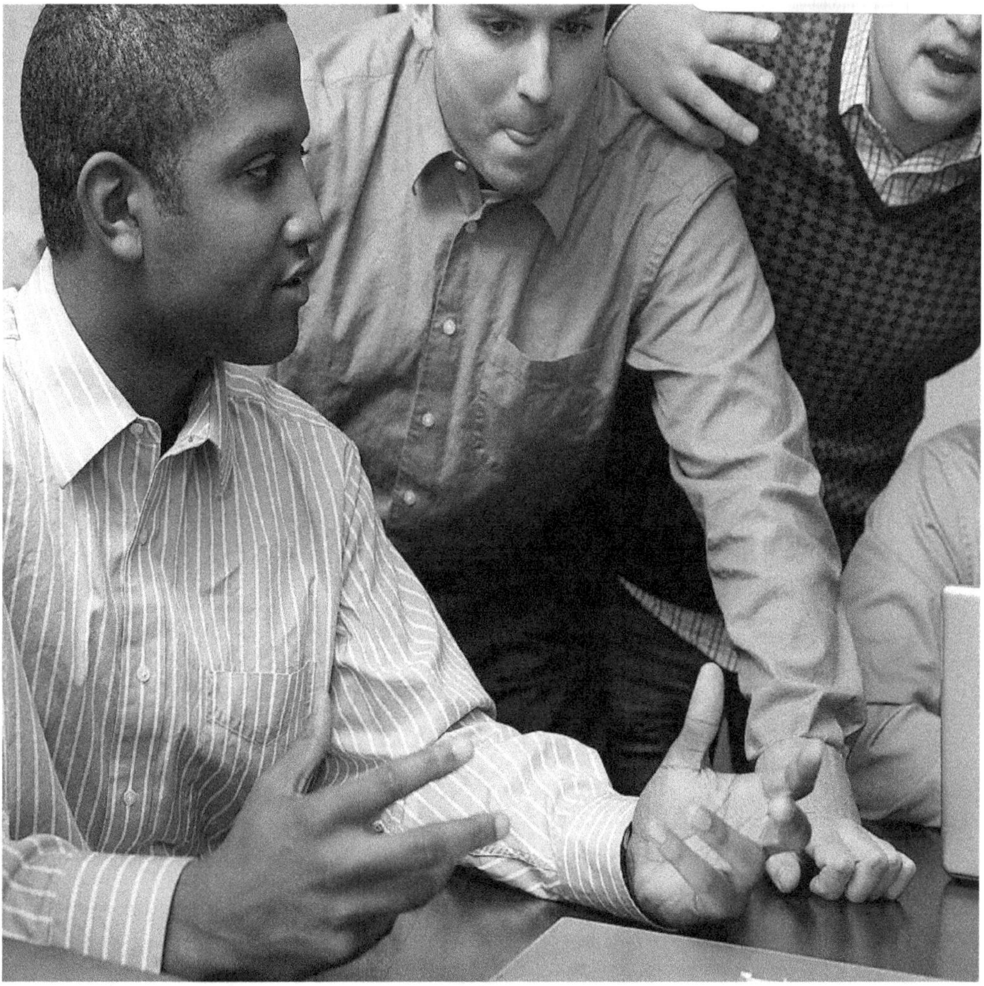

You & Your Team

Reverend Mike Wanner

Your Team is You, Your Prison & Maybe A Technology Partner

Copyright

October 11, 2017

Reverend Mike Wanner

Selected Images Used by License

Table Of Contents

Table Of Contents 3
Introduction 4
1 - The Delay 5
2 - Segmentation For Rehabilitation 7
3 - What Is A Joint Venture 8
4 - What A Joint Venture Could Offer 11
5 - Business Better Than A Low Wage Job 12
6 - Better Family Reconnection 14
7 - Better Spouse Support 15
8 - Aligning With A Higher Purpose 16
9 - The Challenge Is To Make It Work 18
10 - Who To Partner With 19
11 - Opportunities Can Change A Lot 20
12 - Key Points About Joint Ventures 21
13 - Starting Your Joint Venture 22
14 - Be Ready For Your Exit! 25
15 - Thank You 26
16 - Don't Worry Ever 27
17 - Resource Books 28
18 - Angels Please Prayers 30
19 - Private Channeling 31
20 - Reverend Mike Wanner 32

Introduction

The topic of segmentation that I have introduced in my last few books is evolving into a series of books that are focused on subtle changes in the dynamics of the way that prisons have developed.

I live in Philadelphia and the history during the early days of Independence here helped formulate prison protocols that aligned with the Divine in theory but in the application may have been less than fully developed.

The Mass Incarceration of recent times clearly indicates that we could benefit from realignment for the future. In 2013, I was invited to channel Angel Raphael, The Angel Of Healing, and that has let to a series of books that seems to talk about some of the human needs that have been too long ignored.

In 2013, Angel Raphael invited me to visit a prison energetically.

"I asked Mike to Step into Prison Energetically

I have asked Mike to get the address and location within a prison of a designated space so he can visit energetically and receive feedback for us. Whether he will have time, interest or opportunity to do this will be interesting to see. As he writes this, he is not thrilled with the idea. We are already consuming a lot of his time."   ARS16

1 - The Delay

While delayed by other books, The invitation was honored in 2016. The following books related to prisons grew out of the invitation stated above:

1. *Angel Raphael Speaks Volume 4: Angels, Addicts, Alcoholics & Prisoners - Oh Yeah!*
2. *Angel Raphael Speaks Volume 5: Prisoners Caring for Alcoholics - Australia In Miniature   Projects Intro*
3. *Angel Raphael Speaks Volume 6: Prisoners Caring for Addicts - Australia In Miniature For   Addicts*
4. *Prison Jobs Now: Providing Care For Addicts And Alcoholics*
5. *Angel Raphael Speaks - Prisons (A Kindle only book -2013)*
6. *Contained Care Communities: Concept*
7. *Australia In Miniature*
8. *Prison Possibilities Dialogue Series: Concept*
9. *Prison Possibilities Dialogue Series: Volume 2 Dialogues*
10. *Prison Possibilities Dialogue Series: Volume 3 Dialogues*
11. *Prison Possibilities Dialogue Series: Volume 4 Dialogues*
12. *Prison Possibilities Dialogue Series: Volume 5 Dialogues*
13. *Prison Possibilities Voluntary Exile: Concept*
14. *Prison Possibilities Correction Coaches: Concept*
15. *Prison Possibilities for Mexicans: Is A Boat Better than A Wall?*
16. *Prison Possibilities Family Time: A Reason to Thrive!*
17. *Prison Genius Pool: "So Much Genius In Jail."*
18. *Prison Possibilities Access Systems: Prisoner Access by Request*
19. *Prisoner's Lawyers Can Save The American Economy: Make A Buck Doing It & Be Thanked!*

20. Prisoner Family Talks, Days, Stays & Vacations: Connecting Helps Healing
21. Prisoner Writing Projects: Write To Heal, Start Over & Reconnect
22. Prison Cell Clearing & Blessing: Clear Entities, Chase Ghosts, and & Create Sacred Space
23. Prisoner Professors: Show You Are Aware Create Change With Care
24. Prison Reiki? Maybe Someday? A Gateway To Help Heal Prisons & America?
25. Judges and An Angel Rule On Possibilities: We Can Cut Sentences & Prison Costs
26. Ideas For Prison Wardens: Leadership Is Not Easy
27. Solitary Community: Could Community Support Cut Costs and Issues?
28. Prisoner Projects Communication Teams: Communications Can Change Lives
29. Motivating & Empowering Prisoners? Invite Prisoners To Find Their Motivation & Their Future
30. Prison Segmentation for Safety
31. Prison Segmentation for Security
32. Dowsing For Prisoners
33. Ex-Prisoners Possibilities with Real Estate Investors
34. Prison Segmentation For Mental Peace

This book continues to carry the potential for rethinking that can help to reduce incarceration to those who we need to have there.

I want to trigger mindset shifts in the prisoners as well as employees and the community. We need a lot more Objective Productive Dialogues about Enhancing the lives of Prison Employees, Prisoners, Taxpayers and the Families of all.

2 - Segmentation For Rehabilitation

It seems that one of the significant obstructions to rehabilitation is the multitude of mindsets that spiral down all potentials. The mindsets seem to be rigidly in opposition to the success of the apparent thought thinker enemy.

The opposition seems to be to anybody and everybody that tries to bring forth a concept for consideration. We have had enough obstruction, thank you.

Let us no longer double down on obstruction to progress. Let us instead double up on listening and selecting things that we can agree upon as helpful.

Prisons are very full, and that adds complexity to efforts to rehabilitate prisoners. Everywhere there are people and no space.

Segmentation adds space, and that can help add options.the option that we want to discuss here is a Joint Venture effort. This could involve the prison, the prisoners and perhaps others.

Others could be sponsoring Non-Profits, Business Partners, Technology Partners, Interested Political Groups, Colleges, and Universities. The latter are ideal partners as they have the wherewithal to intellectually develop the seeds of new thought that could add tremendous potential.

3 - What Is A Joint Venture

The term joint venture (JV) can mean different things to different people. For concept purposes, I will share the idea and defer any legal entity structure questions for professional definition.

A JV could be a business entity established by two or more parties characterized by shared functions and ownership, pooled returns and risks, and shared authority.

Typically, efforts are initiated for one or more purposes which may include:
1. To open a new unestablished market
2. To gain operating efficiency
3. To share risks for significant investment
4. To combine skills and capabilities

Most joint ventures may be incorporated, but some may be unincorporated and actually may appear as little more than a specific operating agreement or collaboration agreement. Professional advice would be needed in defining any structure that could be controversial as "An Ounce of Prevention is better than a pound of cure" (anon.)

The goal is to accomplish specific results which either party would deem too risky to start by themselves. The arrangement could be a temporary or long range.

While the prison and the prisoner are pivotal to a successful Joint Venture, there could also be a dynamic expertise benefit to a technical partner that provides both a communication bridge and a professional expertise resource.

The benefit to the technical partner could be a reduced cost employee team that does not require the traditional benefits that workplace staff would and also may be incrementally initiated at a slower pace than a regular startup.

This is not to suggest the JV partners would be avoiding their normal business development but to indicate that new business creation could be deliberately started in a progressive way to add further business efforts that could stabilize their business to benefit the partner and also their main employee base.

The reduced cost employee team cost reference does not suggest the prisoner partner employee would be paid super low wages like prisoners contracted out to corporations. It does indicate however that the prisoners may be paid a fee that is above minimum wage and less than the establish professional partner norm so that all partners have the success of the Joint Venture be more likely to succeed.

The Joint Venture agreement should be explicit about the possibilities for the prisoner joint venture partner to move forward with any agreed employment with the technical partner. The deal could provide for a similar hour commitment upon reentry to that which is comparable to the hours worked while incarcerated.

Prisoner partners should be cautious to be realistic with their expectations about employment and their contribution to the Joint Venture effort. Every prison will likely have a variable ability to host a program of this nature and the primary benefit to the prisoner partner may provide a future foothold headstart to personal self-sufficiency.

Prisoner partners may find it helpful to define the skills they had before a Joint Venture. Awareness of new opportunities that may come up is encouraged.

Raising one's vibration to thoughts of empowerment can be transformative. Prisoners could pray to your God, grow to your potential, flow to the world, show all you can do and go to your optimal level of being.

I would like to quote Jean-Luc Picard, a fictional <u>Starfleet</u> officer in the <u>*Star Trek*</u> franchise created by George Lucas, who said – "Make It So!"

4 - What A Joint Venture Could Offer

Joint ventures in business can be very productive as they allow efforts that would otherwise not be feasible. Joint Ventures in prison could be entirely different but offer many benefits there also.

The separation of one or more prisoners for periods of time where they are isolated from the interference of the general community can be most helpful. Dense human space occupancy can lead to an on-guard defensive posturing which might not allow prisoners to tap into their highest potential.

Between adults and especially men there can be a perceived need to show off and raise the opinions of others by demonstrating skills and abilities. While this can be entertaining, the audience in prison can be distracted from using their precious time to develop the skills that can return them to society and their families.

Segmentation can be much more beneficial to prisoners when they can hear themselves think and begin to work on projects that can make a difference for themselves, their families the prisons and the taxpayers.

A Joint Venture between a prison, one or more prisoners, and others can provide a new foundation on which real rehabilitation can take shape. Repeating the word rehabilitation does not change anything but a great plan, a good team and a lot of hard work can bring an idea to life and many lives to the fulfillment of their potential and deliver many to freedom.

5 - Business Better Than A Low Wage Job

Picking the right structure could allow a prisoner to create a job for when they re-enter into the community. Plan developers would be wise to structure any agreements where many prisons and prisoners and as many others as possible could participate as often as possible during their term of incarceration.

Some prisoners may stay incarcerated forever but some will leave and have a job to take home with them can be a proactive effort to make sure they are much less likely to return.
For the ones that stay forever, a proactive effort can make sure that they are able to help support their families.

With proper structure, a Joint Venture could survive the incarceration, eliminate the Prison's participation and increase the benefits to the then ex-prisoner and any other JV participants. In this scenario, the taxpayers have already benefitted from the income during the incarceration and will also be helped by the increased likelihood that there will not be a returning discharged former prisoner.

The prisoner JV partner will also be less likely to cause trouble while still in prison, be less likely to be in conflict with other prisoners while there, will be less likely to be hurt by other prisoners while in segmentation, and be much more cooperative while having a purpose and a plan for the future.

Low wage prisoner contract jobs would not compare favorably to the potential of a Joint Venture which could really be helpful to family connectivity and support.

The real power in the Joint venture can be the preparation for the Prisoner Reentry into the community with ease and employment and readiness and acceptance.

One of the single most important issues for prisoners returning to the community is their ability to support themselves and their families. If they bring their own job home with them, then they are already ahead of most other Prisoners reentering who have no resources to support themselves.

6 - Better Family Reconnection

Picking the right structure for a JV in segmentation could allow a prisoner to create a job for themselves that also will enable them to support their families while still in prison and reestablish the bonds between parents and children.

Income can make a real difference in the lifestyles of all. If the same prisoner was earning a meager wage in a prison contract job, the family outside would need to focus on survival, and there may be less connectivity with the prisoner.

If a Joint Venture prisoner is able to afford frequent communication, the here and now and also the future could be much more family focused and provide support for each member of the family and their interconnectedness.

Children grow up fast and the loss of bonding time each day may never be recoverable in the long term. Little things do make a big difference in life so reconnecting with a child can make a substantial improvement to the whole family.

The reconnection is of paramount importance to any child who needs their parent. Growing up can be tough without one or both parents.

While a child is growing, the absence of a parent can negatively impact their ability to focus in school and stay out of trouble. Just knowing that a parent is doing better and learning and growing may give some children enough hope to impact their grades positively and consequentially their whole life.

7 - Better Spouse Support

Spouses of prisoners who may never get a break can be encouraged by a joint venture glimmer of hope for better tomorrows, and that may make a tremendous difference. Joint ventures that are successful could strengthen spousal connections further and go a long way.

The prison experience is a real struggle for a spouse even on the best of days. A successful Joint venture could allow prisoners to provide a little better support and more frequent communication.

While money can help, the positivity of the joint venture could remind prisoners that their spouses need to be appreciated respected and treasured.

Besides what the prisoner says to the spouse, what the prisoner tells the children about the spouse and about respecting the spouse is very important.

Children listen to the parents and what the parents say even when it seems that they do not. Be careful to mention loving things about your spouse even when you have frustration over other things about your situation.

Segmentation and the ability to talk freely can contribute to revelations about the relationships of others with their spouses. Individuals can develop an understanding of how better to appreciate, communicate, interact with and show recognition for their partners.

8 - Aligning With A Higher Purpose

Angel Raphael in Message Set 10 had a lot to say about the importance of purpose to the life of a prisoner. Here it is:

"Prison Rehabilitation

The answer to prison rehabilitation is the purpose. While some institutions may have initiated programs to engage their residents, the feeling of a purposeful life brings a new reality to the incarcerated.
Purposes for consideration will be ones that work for the incarcerated as well as the society which actually pays the bills. Unique characteristics to include would be the creation of a feeling of accomplishment generated by prisoner effort and drastic cost savings for the institution.

The real loss to prisons is wasted time, no productivity and no graciousness of interactive genius. If invited, the right use of time can provide different results than now seen.

There is no profit to society when cruelness is applied to the control of citizens. There may be temporary security, but that comes at a significant price to the potential of all.

The best way to learn about what is possible is to listen to the troubled stories of the incarcerated people. Their genius can be tapped by mining information about how to fill the gap that they slipped in to so that newer walkers on their path can find the void filled by their charity of sharing their pain as a love patch to the sinkholes of society.

The answers through this channel are coming differently than most could conceive and that is because neither you nor I have a job whose agenda has its own needs.

You ask to imagine how much can be cut from prison costs to maintain security, improve lives, create a new industry and improve the focus, flavor, and flair of American life and you dowsed for an answer. You got 47% reduction, and you questioned your dowsing. Your questioning is wise because there is a huge industry that has roots in the status quo.

While that is true, your answer has potential that will serve the ones that would resist the initiatives that flow from the message. Their positions are survivable as is for a time unknown but their openness to change can also serve their security.

The change will happen even if they choose to use their money to resist the inevitable avalanche of change. Their opportunities are paramount in the areas of personal safety for all and the possibility to create new meaningful arrangements that are self-sustaining for all levels of the resident base and those employed in the industry."   ARS 10

9 - The Challenge Is To Make It Work

When you find purpose in your life and partners, you can see your peace in a natural way. Segmentation can be the perfect place for your plan to develop so that possibilities are not stifled.

The success of your JV program will depend on your purpose, initiative, starting plan and diligence. Nobody can or will do it for you, and the right matching of partners and opportunities will be essential if success is to be realized.

The combination potentials to benefit many individuals and the facility have great potential but will need sophisticated effort to maximize the benefits. Early participants in each prison may have much more opportunity than spectators.

Prisons are controlled by many different government agencies in the various locations, and there are a lot of historical precedents which has formed the rules of what presently exists. Early participants may have some opportunities to create new criteria for the prisoners of the future.

You can explore possibilities by asking for helpful ideas, discussing them in detail, finding opportunities for others to participate, being diligent and inclusive, and documenting it all.

After a solid draft is done, you can share it and ask for suggestions that can take you further. Considering all ideas can be tremendously helpful in carrying your project to the levels of success that you envision. If you stay humble and inclusive, success will be more likely.

10 - Who To Partner With

Prisons are typically crowded, and the intensity of human emotions could be detrimental to the most vulnerable in the crowd.

Stressed individuals do not always realize why they are stressed but the intensity of stress is prevalent throughout the country, and it is a frequent topic of business conversation.

I have a whole website devoted to stress, and you can visit it at http://www.StressReleaseCoach.com . That material and more is included in a book that I wrote called *Stress Release Energy Work: How To Cope* which is available on Amazon and Kindle

Ratcheting down the intensity of prison through segmentation could go a long way to help mitigate stress induced crises. The damage of the whole incarceration experience will not fade as quickly as stress can when you are proactive.

While Segmentation can help stabilize the living space for all and spread out the use, so all do not feel as crowded, your initiative will be needed if you want to take charge of the present and your future.

You will need to build a team, and it will need to be multi-faceted and multi-functional so that you can prepare to develop the service that you wish to offer.

It is simple enough to talk about the peace that can flow from spaciousness while mentioning the advantages of segmentation for the freer settling of emotional charges but doing takes work.

11 - Opportunities Can Change A Lot

Your mind can filter things out or allow them into your life. Participants are invited to create choices for everybody.

You are a powerful being even if you have been broken by your life circumstances or any of the events that occurred since your birth. The simple little powerful tool that can help you begin a new journey of personal discovery is the purpose.

As you treat yourself more kindly and spread the impact of your kindness to other beings on the planet, your state of living will morph into a potential that you have not even dreamed possible. That new vision of possibility can take you into a feeling of vulnerability that is new and fresh and maybe even scary.

While that may sound exciting or ominous, the reality is that it may merely be an unknown experience.

Please be diligent about doing your homework so that you can quantify the unknown and can assess, evaluate and develop your concerns into a future that can unfold as you have prepared for it.

You can continue to dig into the details as you go and you might be delighted with what happens as you refocus, refine and shift.

12 - Key Points About Joint Ventures

1. While your experience in prison may be less than pleasant, your experience is part of your awareness, and it may have information that can be used where you are now and where you will be in the future.

2. If you use everything that you know, your ability to serve many people will be more significant than if you pick the same target market like everybody else.

3. Additionally, consideration should be given to target a slice of the pie that is attainable.

4. Your negative life experiences could be a benefit when you are applying to defend a potential target from people who do what you previously did before you decided to move in a positive direction. Knowledge is power, and a criminal past could be a credential that shows you the vulnerability for a business's security

5. Your potential service to others will be most beneficial if you can be smart about avoiding competition with others who have a better success record.

6. Select a niche you can serve now and later.

7. Avoid competition by being wise and doing what few others are doing, are likely to do or even want to do. A minuscule monopoly can ensure your future lock on a segment of the market that you own.

13 - Starting Your Joint Venture

Your Joint Venture will be contingent upon you putting it all together, applying for a segmented slot and then being diligent about moving forward.

You will have a lot of work to do to get this all going if you really want to do it. Be prepared to think on your feet because being early to an opportunity may bring you the chance but it also will bring a lot of work.

This is not the kind of project that you will succeed at casually. A common suggestion for new businesses is the development of a business plan, and that would be an excellent idea for anyone who is interested in doing a joint venture.

There once was a bank in my hometown that declared that "Wishing Won't Do It But Savings Will." If a Joint venture seems right for your future, then it might be a good idea to consider a variation of that saying that might declare that "Wishing Won't Do It but Research, Preparation and Diligence Will."

Please know that I am planting seeds that can grow in many different ways and some may offer you more opportunity than others. As an outsider, it all seems to make sense, but the devil is always in the details.

The initial research would need to be about the policies of the facility where you live and if they embrace segmentation or resist it. New ideas can bring results, but they can also bring complications.

The starting point is to ask some questions about the project and jot down your initial reactions.

Ask yourself:

Who?_____

What?_____

When?_____

Where?_____

How?_____

Why?_____

Then consider what happens if any of the above do not line up. Do You Have a B Plan? Ask yourself:

Who?_____

What?_____

When?_____

Where?_____

How?_____

Why?_____

I do not know enough about any particular prison or prisons in general, so Please proceed with caution!

1. Research
2. Preparation
3. Diligence
4. Analysis
5. Teambuilding
6. Double Checking
7. Work
8. Success

14 - Be Ready For Your Exit!

Build A Job

In Prison

And

Take It Home With You

So You Can

Get Out,

Eat Regularly,

Feed Your Family,

And Stay Out!!!

15 - Thank You

For
Considering
These
Ideas

16 - Don't Worry Ever

Ever

It Does Not Help Prayer Still Does!

Resource: http://www.Create-A-Prayer.com

17 - Resource Books

Books by Rev. Mike at www.Amazon.com

Veterans Healing Six Pack
1. Trauma Healing Options for VA Hospitals: Help for Veterans to Own Their Healing and their future.
2. Trauma Healing Action Steps for Veterans: Help to Start Healing
3. Trauma Healing Action Steps for Veterans: Empowerment
4. Trauma Healing Action Steps for Veterans: Forgiveness
5. Trauma Healing Action Steps for Veterans: Thought Freedom
6. Tea For Veterans: Welcome One Home

PTSD Power Pack:
1. The PTSD Project: Turn Pain To Power
2. PTSD & Soul Retrieval: Putting One Back Together
3. PTSD & The Purple PAD: Calling all Scientists and PTSD Patients

Angel Raphael Speaks Volume 1: Take Courage! God Has Healing in Store for You!
Angel Raphael Speaks Volume 2: Take Courage! God Has Healing in Store for You!
Angel Raphael Speaks Volume 3: Take Courage! God Has Healing in Store for You!
Angel Raphael Speaks Volume 4: Angels, Addicts, Alcoholics & Prisoners – Oh Yeah!
Angel Raphael Speaks Volume 5: Prisoners Caring for Alcoholics - Australia In Miniature Projects Intro
Angel Raphael Speaks Volume 6: Prisoners Caring for Addicts - Australia In Miniature For Addicts
Reiki Journaling from Japan
Reiki Is Alive: God's Great Gift
Four Parts to Healing
Distant Healing: We Are All Connected
Stress Release Energy Work: How To Cope
Does Reiki Love Heal Cancer?
Group Consciousness
Salute To Philadelphia VA Medical Center: Thank You
Reiki Transcript for Reiki 2 & 3 Channels: Dr. Usui Is That You?
God Bless Kindle & Amazon
Puppies Are Different From People
If Your Dog Dies
Toy Guns Are Obsolete
Great Spirit Made Children With Red Skin: AND
The Cage of Fear: Is Not Locked
God Made Children Red, Yellow, Brown, Black & White: Greet Each Child With Kindness

Emergency Medical Kindness In The Cradle Of Liberty: Big City - Cracked Bell
Angels Are Always Around Addicts and Addicts: Help Is Near Now! Invite It In!
Angels Are Always Around Addicts and Alcoholics: Volume 2 - Tools To Help Re-Light Your Life
Prison Jobs Now: Providing Care For Addicts And Addicts
Controlled Care Communities Concept
Prison Possibilities Dialogue Series: Concept
Prison Possibilities Dialogue Series: Volume 2, 3, 4, 5 Dialogues
Prison Possibilities Voluntary Exile
Prison Possibilities Corrections Coaches
Prison Possibilities For Mexicans: Is A Boat Better Than A Wall?
Prison Possibilities Family Time: A Reason to Thrive!
Prison Genius Pool: "So Much Genius In Jail."
Prison Possibilities Access Control: Prisoner Access by Request
Prisoner's Lawyers Can Save The American Economy: Make A Buck Doing It & Be Thanked!
Prisoner Family Talks, Days, Stays & Vacations: Connecting Helps Healing
Prisoner Writing Projects: Write To Heal, Start Over & Reconnect
Prison Cell Clearing & Blessing: Clear Entities, Chase Ghosts, and & Create Sacred Space
Prisoner Professors: Show You Are Aware Create Change With Care
Prison Reiki? Maybe Someday? A Gateway To Help Heal Prisons & America?
Judges and An Angel Rule On Possibilities: We Can Cut Sentences & Prison Costs
Ideas For Prison Wardens: Leadership Is Not Easy
Solitary Community: Could Community Support Cut Costs and Issues?
Prison Project Communications Team: Communications Can Change Lives
Motivating & Empowering Prisoners? Invite Prisoners To Find Their Motivation
Prison Segmentation For Safety, And Sanity, Security, Peace, and Space
Prison Segmentation For Security
Dowsing for Prisoners; Answers from Above
Ex-Prisoner Possibilities With Real Estate Investors
Prison Segmentation For Mental Peace

Little Books at Kindle.com by Rev. Mike:
English Medical History Questionnaire For Non-English Speakers
English Language Helper For Non-English Speakers
Wise Wonderful Women Are The Well Of The Family
Answers for Test & Research: Dowsing Power
Crisis? Reiki! Baby? Reiki!
Bible References For Healing
Angel Raphael Speaks – Prisons
Angel Raphael Speaks – Veterans
The Saint Off Interstate 95

18 - Angels Please Prayers

Addict's

Angels of Healing Selected
Help Me to Stay Directed
Come To Me From The Sky
I Am Ready to Succeed Not Try
If I Don't Invite You In
I Might Not Win
I Have Been Lost For Too Long
Help Me To Stay Strong

Alcoholic's

Angels of Healing On High
Help Me to Stay Dry
Come To Me From The Sky
I Am Ready to Succeed Not Try
If I Don't Invite You In
I Might Not Win
I Have Been Lost For Too Long
Help Me To Stay Strong

From

http://AngelRaphaelSpeaks.com/AAAAAAA/

19 - Private Channeling

Angel Raphael Speaks a series of free messages that are channeled through Reverend Mike Wanner for the Highest good and Highest Healing of all concerned.

Many questions arise about Reverend Mike doing private channeling, and he does help with that so e-mail him.

Reverend Mike is available worldwide as a psychic channel, emotional release facilitator, spiritual energy practitioner & teacher, and public speaker. He looks forward to meeting you soon!

Email - mikewann@voicenet.com 215-342-1270 PRIVATE SPIRITUAL READINGS/channelings or Spiritual Healing Sessions: Telephone or in person. Rev. Mike is available for private, one-on-one intuitive sessions with you, his Guide Family, and your Guides. He helps by offering clarity on emotional situations about your life, your purpose, your spirituality, and the release of stuffed emotions and cellular memory.
Connect to the love of your Guides today!
Contact Rev. Mike for an appointment.

Sessions available:

Spiritual Readings
Angel Channeling
Distant Reiki Healing
Remote Clearing of Stuffed Emotions
Distant Clearing Cellular Memory
Distant Clearing Energy Blockages
+Remote Clearing of the Chakras
Customized needs
Mastermind dowsing responses to yes/no direction finding questions.

Rev. Mike is a facilitator of healing. He brings you and the Divine together so that you can align with the Divine and have a great time and a great life. All healing is between you and God, as it should be. Go ahead and start without Rev. Mike. Visit his prayer site http://www.Create-A-Prayer.com. Take the first step NOW.

20 - Reverend Mike Wanner

Rev. Mike Wanner started his Metaphysical and Ministerial studies with Reiki in 1993 and had studied seven styles of Reiki in the U.S., Japan, Canada, Denmark and Australia. He is certified to teach. He became certified to teach Integrated Energy Therapy in 1999 and co-taught the first IET class of the new Millennium. Mike began dowsing in 2001.

Ordained as a Metaphysical Minister of the International Metaphysical Ministry and an Interfaith Minister of the Circle of Miracles Ministry, Rev. Mike practices and teaches spiritual energy therapies in the Philadelphia Area.

Rev. Mike holds ministerial degrees from the University of Metaphysics and the University of Sedona. He is a Pastoral Care Associate of Aria - Frankford Hospital. He taught at the National Academy of Massage Therapy and Health Sciences.

Rev. Mike was a faculty member of the Medical Mission Sister's Center for Human Integration's School of Integrated Body/Mind Therapies in Fox Chase, Philadelphia, PA for twelve years.

Rev. Mike is licensed by the teaching of Intuitional Metaphysics to practice Spiritual Healing and Scientific Prayer. Mike is also a Prayer therapist.

Rev. Mike was elected in 2007 to the status of "Fellow of the American Institute of Stress."

In 2008, Rev. Mike became a practitioner of Coincidental Recognition as he incorporated the CoRe System into his spiritual healing practice.

In 2009, Rev. Mike trademarked a new healing process called Quantum Quatro! Subtle Energy System Support®.

In 2011, Rev. Mike joined the outreach program known as the Health Advantage Group.

In 2012, Rev. Mike became a Certified Professional Coach by The Master Coaching Academy and Joined the Personal Empowerment Group.

Before his Metaphysical, Ministerial and Coaching studies, Rev. Mike worked for Sears Roebuck and Co. while in High School and after graduation, until he joined the U. S. Air Force in 1965. He returned to Sears from Vietnam in 1969 and stayed until 1978. His final Sears assignment was as an efficiency expert in Methods - Operational Research and Development.

He volunteered with Burholme Emergency Medical Services from 1969 and is still a Life Member and Board of Directors Member. He started a private ambulance company in 1975 and worked professionally in the field until 2001 when he devoted his full attention to real estate investing, healing, coaching, and writing.

May All Who Read This Be Blessed
AND SO IT IS!

www.ingramcontent.com/pod-product-compliance
Lightning Source LLC
Chambersburg PA
CBHW050035230526
45470CB00003B/1296